Praise for Jennifer Lagier's book, *Harbingers*:

"With keen and loving attention to the natural world, Jennifer Lagier writes poems that reroute you for the better. "Dive into the white rush/ of uncertain currents." These poems bring me up close to the world's uncertainties, yet they don't push me under, rather make me grateful for Lagier's clear-eyed vision and feeling more able to cope with the unpredictable, not only in nature but in the whole of life. She gives me faith that though "shaken and surprised/ on an alien shore," we may weather the difficulties by turning toward and not away from them."

—Patrice Vecchione, Author of *Step into Nature: Nurturing Imagination & Spirit in Everyday Life* and *The Knot Untied: Poems*.

"While many of the poems in *Harbingers* explore environmental issues, particularly the drought that has plagued California, they also engage the human equation—how one can live in a changing world. The first poem in this stunning collection concludes, "why precision matters." It is exactly that quality of precision—visual, empathetic, linguistic—that elevates these poems to the category of the unforgettable."

—Joan Colby, Author of *Ribcage*,
Senior Editor of FutureCycle Press

"In *Harbingers*, by Jennifer Lagier, you will find the sharp eye of the photographer, the passion of the environmental activist, and a prayer for the survival of the Earth. As the poet takes you on coastal walks on the Monterey Peninsula, she reveals her delight in all natural things and her fears about global warming. Elegantly crafted poem jewels, a joy to read."

—Diane Frank, Author/Editor of *River of Earth and Sky: Poems for the Twenty-First Century;*
Author of *Swan Light*, and *Yoga of the Impossible*

"Jennifer Lagier, in her new book of poems, *Harbingers,* is sojourner par excellence, seeking signs and transporting the reader to her beloved California. A refugee from flat land and farming, her "Adaptation" is complete to the "curved, peninsula dunes, restored missions, sea lion laden piers, and oceanic lagoons." In this masterful collection, Lagier is witness to global warming, laments a place more and more alien, where a "persistent high pressure ridge reroutes the rain." An avid environmentalist, the author uses muscular language, vividly describing the effects of global warming—a burning horizon, a hot rising ocean, denuded forests, crumbling beaches, and king tides. Yet a recurring theme also runs through this extraordinary collection—gratitude. Lagier rejoices in the land's beauty, in friendship, in poetry. In her use of rich, compelling language, fine-tuned sensibilities and sensitivities, the book provokes questions, engages the reader in meaningful dialogue. *Harbingers* is a book not to be missed."

—Mary Jo Balistreri, Author of *Joy in the Morning* and *Gathering the Harvest.*

"Jennifer Lagier ends the first poem in *Harbingers,* with a foretelling and instructive discovery, "why precision matters." We have a marriage of perception and anticipation throughout each page of her journeys of soul and self, which is, for this fine poet, Mother Earth. Her full moon "spills sparkling gold across dimpled water." Jennifer's strength always is the potential—"I glean metaphors from dying vines."

—Gordon Preston, Author of *Pieces of Monterey Bay*

HARBINGERS

JENNIFER LAGIER

BLUE LIGHT PRESS ❖ 1ST WORLD PUBLISHING

1st WORLD
PUBLISHING

SAN FRANCISCO ❖ FAIRFIELD ❖ DELHI

1ST WORLD LIBRARY
PO Box 2211
Fairfield, IA 52556
www.1stworldpublishing.com

BLUE LIGHT PRESS
www.bluelightpress.com
Email: bluelightpress@aol.com

BOOK & COVER DESIGN
Melanie Gendron
www.melaniegendron.com

FIRST EDITION

Library of Congress Control Number: 2016946251

ISBN 9781421837598

HARBINGERS

CONTENTS

Acknowledgments

These poems, some in other versions, have appeared in the following journals and anthologies: *Book Movie, Centrifugal Eye, Conceit, Crab Fat Literary Magazine, Cyclamens & Swords, Dead Snakes, Green Fuse, The Guidebook: A Poetry Journal, Haunted Waters Press, Kentucky Review, Medusa's Kitchen, Miller's Pond, Monterey Poetry Review, Painting the Eucalyptus Midnight, Ping Pong: A Literary Journal, Poetry Pacific, Rockford Review, Song of the San Joaquin, Third Wednesday.*

"I am a fugitive and a vagabond, a sojourner seeking signs."
—Annie Dillard, *Pilgrim at Tinker Creek*

for Laura & Kate, my fellow vagabonds

Lower Santa Rosa Creek Trail

Composted pathway curls beneath shadow.
Angular willows intertwine skinny fingers,
form a meandering, secretive tunnel.

Creek puddles ferment
in shallow peat pools
behind emerald kudzu curtain.

I am a noisy, intrusive Goliath,
heavy footfalls scattering
frantic brown sparrows.

Triumphing over gravity,
I ascend to grassy ridge,
panoramic vista of wrinkling ocean.

Elevation leads me onto a deer trail
into dusty forest, past piles of pine cones.
Skunk scent suggests a long-gone attacker.

I teeter through poison oak thickets,
imagine the metaphor, expense of a stumble,
why precision matters.

Moss Landing in Moonlight

As autumn sun melts,
pink and gold slide into chill,
opaque ocean.
Otters and harbor seals vanish,
replaced by incoming kayakers.

Fishermen reel in tensile lines,
ice their catch, return to safe harbor.
Full moon floats above Elkhorn Slough,
spills sparkling gold across dimpled water.

UNDERTOW

Dive into the white rush
of uncertain currents, abandon
deliberate itineraries, give ourselves
over to gold sunrise, whirling spindrift,
refreshed sands, unfamiliar trails,
new year's siren song.

Let the undertow take us
wherever it chooses.
Drag us over the brink,
far beyond familiar landfall,
past what we have known,
to deposit us, shaken and surprised
on an alien shore.

Harbingers

Strange, premature spring—
blackbirds macraméd
among stark limbs of dormant elm
like ebony beads.

Mornings begin with a light show—
peach and purple infuse drifting fog banks.
Rising sun softens, a celestial blood orange.

Confused plum trees absorb false cues
from unseasonal warmth,
exude pink blossoms.
Buckeyes accelerate from fall into summer.

No rain grail to save us from a cloudless horizon.
The Fisher King lingers, caught in a coma.

Last Stand

Cypress trees stand despite scarred trunks,
wind-amputated crowns,
wrenched away branches.

Azure horizon backlights rooted captives.
Sunrise catches septuagenarians
clumped together on ridgeline.

Interwoven remnants of dwindling forest,
a fallen tangle of toppled limbs
curls around tall survivors.

Downhill, clear cut ruin.
Twisted fingers plead for reprieve,
invoke vanquished spirits of Druids.

Masks

Deceptive sunlight masks frosty wind gusts.
Blue shadows beneath pine trees
harbor faux snowfall.
White encrusts wooden bridge planks,
sparkles from frozen foliage.

Chill blows inland, across hills.
Polar vortex penetrates mittens.
Aching knuckles, cold fingers.
Mud trails stiffen.
Iced puddles harden.

Weather patterns shift.
Glaciers, permafrost melt.
Scientists predict
a wild winter El Niño
as hot oceans rise.

High Pressure Wild Card

Rain clouds hit an atmospheric wall,
dump drizzle on Vancouver,
snow in Chicago.

Along Monterey Bay, parched chaparral
and shriveled sage concede the battle.
Storm tides slam ashore, ignorant
of faux spring, this year's tardy winter.

Befuddled plums erupt, bare limbs
concealed within festive blossoms.
Hillsides release lupine and poppies into dry shrouds.
Wild grasses bleach blonde before our very eyes.

It's rumor and sun glow,
a persistent high pressure ridge
rerouting downpour.

DUNES AT DUSK

I stand on ribbed dunes, surrounded
by violet sea, keening gulls,
admire intense purple-orange sky,
triangular sails pushed by wind,
black silhouettes against burning horizon.

It's the lavender hour:
distorted sun in nocturnal descent,
pink tide, bleeding clouds,
jagged gold ribbon
etched across rocking water.

Torch Lilies

Torch lilies glow fiery
in bright morning sun,
exude dripping nectar,
attract hummingbirds and bees.

Red hot pokers tenaciously
adhere to rocky shore,
a scarlet parenthesis
framing monolith stone.

Gulls find no hospitable perch
upon their barbed fronds.
Squirrels seek refuge beneath
silver succulent forts.

Cactus sentinels lift
notched bayonets to sky,
warn away walkers
with smoldering blooms.

At dusk, burning scepters
border a winding trail,
guide coastal deer,
pariah wanderers home.

ADAPTATION

I am a flatland, peach ranch refugee,
relocated to curved, peninsula dunes,
restored missions, commercial fishing boats,
sea lion laden piers, oceanic lagoons.

Back in Escalon, I raised sweet corn,
tomatoes, melons and squash.
On Marina shores, brisk wind wilts roses,
snaps fragile foxgloves.
Weather is cold, water rationed.

Acreage is expensive, unattainable,
tiny houses packed cheek to jowl.
Twisted cypress cling to jagged coastline.
Pets snarl at raccoons and deer.

Each day, I revel in rafts of sleeping otters,
somersaulting dolphins, wise-cracking gulls.
Transplanted roots sink deep, keep me stable.
Friendships, poetry blossom; this is my home.

Last Flash

Sun melts into a deformed pat of butter,
drips below fog belt,
slides toward purple ocean.

Inflamed horizon reddens
as torched clouds transform:
pink, lavender, golden.

Rorschach fire ball
hangs just above dunes,
gray chaparral, rows of bristling artichokes.

Slowly, engorged light sack descends.
Illumination sizzles against distant surf.

With a final flash,
day disappears, night begins—
navy sky, icy moon, burning stars.

Bluff

Afternoon disperses morning fog.
Biting breezes gust inland from ocean.

Gulls skid across bright sky as rogue wind
blusters petals from yarrow and poppies.

Bare beach, minus tourists, a gold backdrop
for twisting sand devils, cartwheeling flotsam.

Don't be fooled by summer's sun,
wet-suited surfers, deceptive blue water.

Seductive California shoreline promises
languid paradise, delivers chill.

Witching Hour

White owls on forked limbs
croon incantations, mesmerize tiny bats
who squeak from the elm tree,
dart among scrub oak and cypress.

Raccoons indulge in petty garbage can thefts.
Raptors soar silently above riddled lawn,
scan for gophers, squirrels
unprotected by burrows.

Wetland mist wraps moon in gauzy haze.
Subtle fog diffuses lunacy.
Brightness reveals wicked deeds
requiring darkness.

HORIZON

Distant headlands jut beyond
kelp-clogged lagoon.
Daredevil terns fling themselves
from bright sky,
dive to cerulean depths in their quest
for anchovies.

Silver and purple fog stacks like parfait
against dry hills of Palo Corona.
Mist rivulets bleed along Carmel River,
shield green-leeched pastures,
grazing cattle from golden sun glare.

Fresh day, unknown trail.
I explore fern canyon,
rickety foot bridge,
give poison oak wide berth.
Path choices—endless.
Destination—uncertain.

October

Sunrise oversleeps.
Pink horizon blooms a bit later each day.
Cypress limbs gesture against
distant blear of gold fog.

Dirt trail bends along bay,
dim above empty beach.
Benches are barely visible,
morning surfers missing.

Sycamores are reduced to rags,
shed ragged leaves.
Cast off foliage exudes spicy scent,
transmutes to humus.

Holly berries—bright embers
among damp evergreens.
Squirrels gather acorns,
prepare for barren months.

One more year depleted.
We hunker down,
lick wounds, count our blessings,
hibernate.

CARMEL RIVER LAGOON

Tethered to habit and a small dog,
I sprint above crumpled beach,
greet morning walkers, floating otters,
egrets wading through grass.

Below me, incensed ocean
slams tumbling wave spume
against sculpted cove,
bronzed, glowing sand.

Among ancient cypress,
sleek blackbirds swivel beady eyes,
reconnoiter picnic scraps,
squawk in gossiping covens.

Beneath burning horizon,
terns flutter, pierce elusive anchovies
within steaming, sheltered lagoon.
Gratitude burgeons; poetry captures.

EGRET

Wild tides fling rogue waves, shredded kelp,
flay broken boulders upon stony beach.

Pelicans skim spindrift, buzz maverick surfers.
A single egret picks apart shattered snails.

Morning precipitates, a gauzy deluge
somewhere between serious shower and mist.

White skies mask atmospheric intentions,
offer no hint of future clearing or sun.

I shelter in warm kitchen, make a fire,
seek metaphors, celebrate seabirds and storm.

WANING

The year wrenches to a chilly close.
Flood tides wax, overtake stony beach.
Summer grasses wither, sere fodder for
grazing cattle on rugged terrain.
Geese consider migration to kinder climes.

We pull on jackets, woolen mittens.
Sunless mornings paint noses red.
Harbor seals are replaced by mating otters,
thrashing castaways within icy surf.

A scrim of stolid fog bank hangs above
stiff cypress, goose pimpled bay.
Reeking wood smoke infuses mist.
Horizons shrink as another year wanes.

Grumpy Old Men

I hear snorting, loud griping and groaning
long before an opening between yuccas
permits me to see three geriatric seals
sprawled atop stony outcroppings.

On the next rock, dark terns unwillingly listen
to a daily litany of moaning geezer complaints
from this trio of chubby curmudgeons.

The splash of incoming tide soaks and disturbs them.
They whine, grumble about what aches,
how they used to command respect.
Now nobody loves them.

Transience

Morning tides wander inland,
change their mind, roll toward
open ocean, carry foam and flotsam
to the depths of blue bay.

Sunlight makes no commitment,
slides between hillsides, fogbanks,
erases ridge tops, distant forest,
comes and goes by transient whim.

I stand near Hurricane Point,
uprooted and uncertain,
ponder future directions,
feel the winds change.

The Blues

Arid land of the abandoned,
forsaken territory.
Mist brings illusion of deliverance,
sterile clouds, mocking fog.

Gulls flap across vacant skies,
pursue pelicans soaring
south past drying tules,
toward a shrunken lagoon.

Empty trail mimics blank sheet,
bare spot in a dying marriage.
Precipitation, vague memory,
as we endure lethal surfeit of sun.

Breaking the Drought

Dry year, we witness termination of optimism,
endure progressive withering,
sere estrangement.

An immoveable high pressure ridge
thickens between us,
creates an unmovable wall.

Parched garden, irrigation denied,
shrivels, deconstructs
to bare ground.

I crave reappearance of moist seasons
not this punitive, sterile spring.

Lead us back from the underworld
with redemptive rainfall thundering down.

Fata Morgana

Storm clouds are merely mirage,
ruddy smears above dark hills,
a yearning wish
meant to thaw cold morning.

We huff along ocean trail,
exhale white exclamations –
two chilly dragons,
fire power snuffed.

Ashen sunlight tricks the eye,
spins the illusion of falling rain
over golden slough, mist enclosed
sycamores, rounded mountain tops.

Temperature drops; small flakes
flurry among subtle drizzle.
Charged air aches to transform
into a blizzard.

Post Drizzle Prism

For months we have begged stubborn heavens to open
forgive us our trespasses, gift us with moisture.
Now, in the aftermath of this season's first downpour,
we are dazzled by drizzle, prismatic reflections.

Sunlight bends around rain, refracts primary colors.
A rainbow hangs against lavender fogbanks.
Beneath its fading arch, a dolphin pod circles,
silver dorsal fins dissecting incoming waves.

Good luck totems dominate hazy horizon,
delight undeterred, morning walkers.
Has drought finally broken?
Is this absolution or brief relief?

Tenacity

Pounding tangles of storm-propelled driftwood.
Freak tsunami tides move assaulted shore inland.

Salt mists, winter winds sculpt ancient cypress
into twisted bonsai survivors.

Carmel River reroutes each spring,
cuts a new channel.

Lagoon waters rise and fall.
Sand bars spread, then diminish.

Stone headlands devolve into tumbles of boulders,
relentless surf grinds broken granite to crystals.

The calm surge of incoming spindrift can be deceptive.
It takes deep roots to avoid being swept away.

WARNING

Crimson patches entwine fallen logs,
embroider forest floor, tawny meadow.

Poison oak raises red flags,
shrieks a colorful warning.

Dogs trot through triangular patches,
transmit tortuous itch to their owners.

Fiery foliage caresses, then scalds.
Ruddy welts blossom.

Scarlet flames lick, then sear bare skin.
Toxic oil torments, burns for hours.

Lunacy

Swollen planet glows, silver-plates
oak forest, floats above pine.

Crows and turkey vultures vanish.
Woodpeckers, silenced by night.

Roof and walls seem claustrophobic.
Darkened patio, honeysuckle arbor invite.

Supermoon awakens odd yearnings,
overwinds the imagination.

Cool sister, shadow doppelganger
of sun, slides across the black sky.

Strut

He's a cocky bastard, full of himself, a fat quail
arrogantly perched on a curved cypress limb,
his flustered, forgotten harem diving for cover
among sage, beach geranium, coast chaparral.

On nearby road, ungracefully aging males
gun red Maseratis, Lamborghinis, Ferraris
troll for trophy wife arm-candy
among anorexic, blonde joggers.

Assets and power jockey for dominance
in pheromone saturated air.
It's an alpha parade, puffed up fowl,
preening men beside turgid bay.

Tectonic

Continental drift grinds granite edges,
elevates adobe bluffs above Pacific Ocean,
ruptures rammed tectonic plates,
leaves behind ragged coastline.

Unstable earth shifts when least expected.
Fissured gullies widen from relentless erosion.
King tides deconstruct stone, clog lagoon,
create beach with minerals transmuted to sand.

Temblors rearrange California,
erase trails, splinter mountains, trigger slides.
Strata shifts beneath our feet;
the entire state wobbles.

SQUALL

All day the sky teases.
Bubbling storm clouds,
then sunlight around dinnertime.
Dark squall finally
blowing in from the ocean.

Gusty deluge whips redwoods
into a drenched frenzy,
rust-colored needles cast down
to become one more startling hue
in a soggy compost pastiche.

Night brings banshee winds
that lift and rattle
windows and shingles,
command a second quilt.

By morning, this cabin,
a water-tight golden ark,
shelters and warms,
offers a good book, a crackling fire,
a hot cup of coffee.

Storm Tide

Slender beach endures wild sea assault.
Impromptu creek beds emerge.
Gouged sand devolves into a showcase
for twisted driftwood, uprooted kelp.

Maverick waves elevate wet-suited daredevils,
fling longboard riders along the taut face
of slippery troughs, past spindrift,
through collapsing tunnels of tumbling surf.

King tides hammer crumbling shoreline,
break against granite boulders, splash salt spray
across cloudy windows of cliff-edge cottages.
Dark shapes huddle before crackling fires.

Above, lightning splinters congested sky,
evokes primitive rituals, cave paintings.
I scribble through brown outs, screaming gales,
rumbling storms.

DIFFUSION

Monochrome morning etches cypress fronds
against tinny horizon, silvery dunes.

Ascending mist hijacks the eye,
swaddles sun within translucent backdrop.

Ragged shoreline lacerates surf swell.
Harbor seals drag themselves onto high ground.

Patrolling pelicans reconnoiter
teeming schools of anchovies.

I wander, pulled by muted radiance,
warming earth, a burning planet's bronze trail.

Surge

Echoes of northern storms pound ashore.
A high pressure ridge impedes needed rain.

Ferocious surf slams sand and stone,
casts wreckage onto gouged beach.

Morning reveals retreating riptides,
tattered kelp, broken sea glass and shells.

Gulls forage among tide pools,
prod, then quarrel over what spoil remains.

Whale flukes erupt from spindrift,
punctuate pink horizon, another dry, golden day.

Waste Land

Shredded fog floats above dying coastline.
Salt mist mocks earth,
no substitute for rainfall.

Deceived fruit trees offer
doomed pink and white blossoms.
Unrelenting sun aggravates parched chaparral.

Soon gardens will become wreckage,
shriveled effigies of what used to be flowers.
Dry hills, lifeless pines become powder keg
tinder for inevitable fire.

We bargain to break the long drought,
implore Demeter to heal our blasted land.
Fill our ponds and rivers!
Bestow a benediction of water!

KING TIDES

January, 84 degrees—winter missing in action.
Persistent drought, freakish heat, substantiate global warming.
King tides, cruel reminder of faraway storms
soaking geography, not California.

Swollen surf sweeps fishermen off coastal boulders,
mesmerizes beachcombers, driftwood collectors.
Engorged ocean glows, pushes itself ashore.
Burnished lagoon floods low-lying wetlands.

Gold sunrise brings no epiphany,
just higher surge, dryer hilltops and meadows.
It's another big buildup—symptoms of tempest
without drenching drama.

Flames

Just before turquoise cove,
red hot pokers plunge flaming fingers
from acacia thickets, gesture toward
gaunt cypress, streaked sky, otter lagoon.

Morning, too bright,
brilliance that blasts, then overwhelms.
Unseasonal sunshine, brassy humidity
make fusty air smolder.

Arid days, sticky nights
stun my imagination.
Roses droop. Azaleas shrivel.
No motivation to scribble or sow.

I long for shaded trails
across secret rivers.

Askew

Nature, out of plumb,
shrinks wetlands, shrivels gardens
of initiative, imagination.

Morning walks bring us eye-to-eye
with thirsty deer, dull-eyed raccoons,
evidence of increased global warming.

Compulsory water rationing is imposed.
Along Ocean Avenue, empty planter boxes,
dying pines, desiccated maples.

Weakened cypress trees topple onto one another—
goliaths so enfeebled by drought and disease,
wind and gravity shove them across Mission Trail.

Skewed season, barren sky,
accelerate freak summer.
Wizened limbs burst with premature blooms.

Code Red

Whales spout off rocky shore,
spew lacy umbrellas against cloudless horizon.

Winding trail along worn adobe bluff
retains shrinking puddles from scant, recent rainfall.

Strange spring bludgeons the coast
with unseasonal hot flash,
pushes puzzled fruit trees into full blossom.

The ocean warms; fish migrate to cooler depths.
Baby harbor seals sicken, die by the hundreds.

Between boulders and sea,
red hot pokers pulse
Planet Earth's emergency signals.

Tanglewood

For a century, storms blow inland,
push against craggy tree trunks,
twist cypress wind breaks
into macraméd love knots.

Scarred limbs form silver lintels,
bracket seascape, reveal spindrift,
dogs barreling across beach
to retrieve red and gold frisbees.

At trail edge, plein-air artists
daub at canvas upon frail easels.
Pollen-rich acacia skirt fallen timber,
paint nearby windshields with a yellow patina.

Gray clouds, smudged fogbanks mingle,
erase morning sun,
offer empty delusions
of imminent downpour.

Illusion

After days of brassy sun,
gloomy morning horizon.
Bronzed estuary mirrors confused charcoal sky.

Heavy fog manifests
delicate chimera of drizzle.
For a few weeks lush hillsides
costume persistent drought with emerald fescue,
golden poppies, yellow acacia.

We tell ourselves meager moisture
will sustain ceanothus, succulents, sea grass.
Mist conjures cruel illusion
of impending rainfall.

Dry Spell

Chill gold hangs within blank sky,
illuminates ashy hilltops,
empty creek beds, dry pastures.

Acidified ocean swooshes
over broken clam shells,
granite boulders,
dwindling beach.

It's a year without wildflowers,
yellowed sea grass
transformed into brittle raffia streamers.

I plod through a repetition of sere days—
blaring sun, shrinking reservoirs,
sterile horizons.

CONTEMPLATION

A lone dreamer meditates above a calm lagoon
as fog cradles hilltops, cloaks far horizon.

She sits cross legged against white sand.
Silver morning, gull cries surround her.

Tranquil surf pulses around jutting stone,
deposits creamy foam along golden shoreline.

Silhouetted observer studies floating kelp beds,
deciphers a tangled raft of snoozing otters.

Black terns plummet from gray sky,
vanish as they puncture still water.

Last Call

Scarred cypress limbs undulate
like silver pythons,
slither from pit viper roots to Medusa crown,
snake toward the sky
along scaly bark.

Maimed trees overlook rising ocean.
Surf gnaws adobe bluff,
reveals shellfish fossils,
buried Esselen grinding stones.

Contemporary artifacts disfigure beach sand:
cigarette butts, plastic shopping bags,
Styrofoam coffee cups, tangle
of fishing line, flip flops.

Wind and tide scatter Trojan Horse
dead carp, deformed waterfowl, strangled lagoon.
We have had our last warning.

Pierced

Malevolent willow punctures calla lily.
Skinny twig protrudes, mirrors erect yellow stamen.

Morning chill pierces, penetrates layers of clothes,
hip joints, stiff knees, arthritic fingers.

Pine needles mingle with rotting wreckage
of toadstools, rubbery mushrooms.

I wander granite trail past faux Tudor cottages.
Jet streams lacerate cloudless horizon.

Gold sun pokes through endless blue
above restless ocean.

ARID SPRING

Shredded fog floats above dying meadow.
Salt mist mocks parched earth
with no substitution for rainfall.

Deceived apple trees offer
doomed pink and white blossoms.
Unrelenting sun seers parched chaparral.

Soon gardens will become gray wreckage,
shriveled effigies of hydrangeas, camellias,
what used to be flowers.

Dry hills, dead pines and cypress—
powder keg forest,
tempting tinder for inevitable fire.

PORTENTS ON THE LEFT COAST

Uncertain morning, as I wander familiar trail.
Grumpy ravens kvetch from Monterey pines.
Above agitated lagoon, unsettled sky simmers.

In Paris, more hostages, bullets vs. opinions.
Here, a debate within myself: stay and accede
to soul-killing beliefs and behaviors?
Or flee on principle without tools to start over?

Murky vista reveals no clues.
I wrestle terror, turmoil, emotions.
Looking forward, only troubled horizons.

From the Lips of an Invisible God

Drought desiccates fertile tomato fields,
shrivels grapevines, withers cherries,
sends honeybees in search of
fruit trees and almonds.

Ponds are reduced to cracked mud,
shrinking puddles.
Receding reserve etches lines into stone,
exposes bare canyon clefts
where there used to be fish
and snow runoff water.

Four years have elapsed
since a normal pattern rainfall.
It teaches us to fear reversion to desert,
remember prayer.

Peekaboo Sun

Ragged mist surrounds solar orb,
congeals against dunes,
paints exposed boulders, low-tide bay
shades of silver and gold.

Fog curls across ridgetops,
caresses arid hills,
bejewels pines and cypress,
drizzles on damp forest floor.

White light and pale blue
taunt from ragged holes
wind has torn
through thunderhead clouds.

Future forecast is uncertain—
prognostications thwarted
by coastal summer's
capricious vapors, tentative sun.

CAMBRIA PINES

The trees are whispering
intimations of rising wind,
cicada symphonies,
drippy incursions of fog.

Ground squirrels patrol parched terrain,
as hikers approach, whistle, sound the alarm.
Jays curse from dusty oaks,
pursue one another into yellowing boughs.

Dry forest creaks in the breeze.
Needles spill from stressed, rusty pines.
Red-headed woodpeckers drill dying limbs,
dismantle diseased wood, fallen logs.

Dawn Over Monterey Bay

Sunrise hangs above tranquil bay,
streaks mist-muddled horizon,
placid cove, with intense solar flare.

Fog shreds drift inland,
diffuse swollen ball
of ascending platinum light.

Below Hopkins Marine Lab,
a grumpy elephant seal
guards his recumbent harem, velvety pups.

Autumn morning slowly unfolds.
I wander Cannery Row,
coffee mug in hand, as coastal deer
forage sand dunes for sea grass.

OCTOPUS

Sunburnt aloes cluster
in tenacious colonies,
protrude from wizened stalks
along ocean bluff.

Rosette tentacles cleave
to dry chaff of previous incarnations,
thrive among broken granite,
rampant hottentot fig.

They cling above placid bay
like scarlet octopi,
starfish swirls, blushing
tumbleweed knots.

TRACES

Big bird has been here
leaving pitchfork footprints across sand,
avian evidence of recent visit, exodus,
hasty airborne departure.

Mysteries deepen.
The usual gulls are absent this morning.
Dispirited blackbirds grumble
as they forage through flotsam.

No pelicans or terns.
Just chill summer, dying pines,
incongruous drought.

Mandala

Omens of pale deer among pines,
jeweled cobweb mandala,
cry of spiraling hawk.

Invisible spider weaves a circular narrative
from secret, subconscious fragments,
cosmic glitter in light.

Trail walker centers, reflects.
Prophet crow rasps approval.
Morning surf whispers, casts spindrift runes

SERENDIPITY

Mist lifts off the Pacific,
leisurely skids across blue sky,
obscures rising sun.

Fog rivulets mesmerize,
flow inland, vaporous neckties
around dry mountain tops.

The trail is mysterious—
winds between kudzu and oak,
disappears within rattlesnake grass.

Found art embellishes forest floor,
a heart-shaped assemblage of pine cones,
prickly valentine beside well-travelled path.

I accept this discovery as good luck omen,
despite scolding squirrels,
screech of spiraling hawk.

Golden Gate Windmill

Silhouetted against curdled sky,
battered arms frozen,
the windmill has been transplanted
from Holland to San Francisco.
It shelters Golden Gate homeless,
our society's Frankenstein monster.

A diaspora of unwanted humans
terrify and haunt us.
The townspeople are subtle—
no pitchforks or torches,
only demands that the destitute
be removed from streets, beaches, sidewalks.

Unmedicated messiahs rave
to crows and passing joggers,
seek refuge with crabs and birds
among dunes, under bushes.

The Blessing

St. Francis stands in a painted garden of Eden,
blesses peacocks, nightingale, dove.
Sheep, goat and frog circle his sandals.
Holiness exudes from psychedelic halo.

The red-headed artist
of Fantastic Oasis
tips a plastic bucket,
hydrates lemon, lavender,
struggling roses.

For a few moments,
the coffee house vanishes.
I pause on the doorstep of paradise.

GLOWER

Spectral sunrise backlights ragged limbs.
Murky sky surrounds granite point,
streaks bronze across silver
cove, choppy lagoon.

Arid spring simmers behind striated fog scrim.
Mist commingles with sterile,
hovering clouds, muddled horizon,
floating layers of pearl, ivory, gray.

Winter segues into soaring temperatures,
another bone-dry, tinderbox summer,
wilted pastures, obsolete lawns.

We resign ourselves to worst-case scenario
as rerouted rain storms snub California.
We implore a higher power to intervene,
lift the curse.

The Hobbit Bench

I wander a meandering trail above glittering ocean,
trudge through dry chaparral, reduced lava dust.

At cliff edge, twisted driftwood
forms a Middle Earth hobbit bench.

Cypress tree stumps, strategic boulders
support a cedar plank.

Braided pew back frames blue sawtooth hills,
flawless azure sky, distant volcanic ridge.

Seductive throne for the hiker
offers unfettered view of pelicans, terns.

Morning walkers wave. Ground squirrels forage.
Passing gulls call. Poetry writes itself.

BEND OVER BACKWARDS

Decades of bowing to strong winds
transform flexibility into permanent distortion.

I am tired of rearranging values and priorities
to create room for unreasonable people.

Relaxing the rules only reinforces bad habits,
sense of entitlement.

Time and travail leave you beaten down,
unable to rise when you need to.

Bending over backwards for those who don't
appreciate sacrifice can make you a cripple.

SUNFLOWERS

Gangly mutants sprout at orchard edge,
proliferate along ditch banks.
Sticky stems bend under the weight
of fried egg center
fringed with bright golden petals.

During the lean years,
I cut handfuls of wildflowers,
displayed them in a mayonnaise jar
circled by yellow pollen
on my red kitchen table.

These were simple times:
innocent blooms,
muscular youth,
uncrushed potential.

Artichoke

Edible flowers at Farmer's Market—
Castroville artichokes piled
in a jaunty green jumble.
Barbed globes conceal
tender hearts inside tough armor.

Pointy leaves mimic a leathery rose,
mature to a thistle.
One careless bobble and sharp thorns
leave painful scars
on an innocent finger.

Hot Flash

Clotted mist rises,
floats like celestial foam
backlights cypress silhouettes.

Morning and I are unsettled,
run hot and then cold.
One minute, my sweatshirt.
In the next, I am struggling uphill,
stripped to sleeveless vest.

The day is uncertain—
promise of glittering bay,
al fresco champagne brunch,
obscured by incoming fog.

Thunderstorm

Thunderheads float above the gold ridgeline,
menace fence posts and metal gate
with jagged splinters of lightning.

Rabbits and raccoons
have taken cover with quail
beneath sage and greasewood.

Prodigal El Niño drags summer storm ashore
with celestial drama, sprinkles overdue rain
on our sizzling doorstep.

Storm Over the Salinas Valley

Silver clouds scud off wild ocean waves,
roll above mustard meadow,
effacing blue mountains.

Storm front whips lettuce fields
as purple sky thickens.
Windmill propellers twirl like a child's pinwheel.

Buffeted grape vines,
splayed against golden slopes,
swing from wooden stakes,
wire gallows.

Field workers, masked by bandanas,
chop weeds despite coming squall,
hoe endless rows of broccoli, zucchini.

Tense horizon splits, dumps thunder,
lightning, finally rain,
answers prayers.

Moon Madness

Silver seeps between cypress fingers,
spills through bedroom window,
voyeuristic light barely dimmed
by remnants of fog.

Full moon makes the sheets itch.
I toss, fidget upon my bed of nails,
a victim of astral lunacy.

Far surf wallops crumbling coastline.
King tides flood
sweet water pond with salty brine,
turn wetland lagoon
into brown, brackish stew.

Shimmering planetoid
hanging above pallid dunes
disorients gravity, dismantles sleep,
arouses a marauding gang
of noisy raccoons.

IMAGINE

I sit above writhing ocean
beneath curdled clouds,
contemplate a fresh start.
I've reinvented myself three times before,
each time vowing it will be the last.
Dog walkers pass and wave.
Squirrels emerge to forage
if I'm still long enough.

How easy and nourishing
to pull up roots,
relocate to a funky bungalow
overlooking forest and sea.
All I require are fireplace,
cozy kitchen, small wooden desk,
perhaps a lover now and then.
My only long-term commitments:
poetry, friends, two spoiled hounds.

Birdman

Asian Art Museum, San Francisco, July 2015

He's my kind of god:
punctual, efficient, polite.
Will fly anywhere,
this world or the next.

Delivers epiphanies, retribution,
announcements of disaster, death.
Claims sold souls from the damned.
Discreetly does whatever you ask.

Deity of the driven,
he lives to perform any dirty deed,
eagerly quivers in anticipation,
bird tail erect.

DEMONIC DUO

Asian Art Museum, San Francisco, July 2015

Don't let cartoon eyes
and toothy smiles fool you.
These soulless, skirted demons
relentlessly track and torment
con men masquerading as victims.
Get on the wrong side of their master,
and they'll transform you to insects.

A former incarnation of myself
must have outraged an Indian god
by eating filet mignon,
drinking too much wine,
refusing to cover my head
inside a temple.
Despite protective art museum glass,
I feel them plotting a take-down,
tracking me as I pause to examine
a multi-armed Vishnu.

Marked, a woman on the run,
I'll be dismembered if apprehended—
payback for irreverence, ritualistic reprisal.

Ganesha

Asian Art Museum, San Francisco, July 2015

Despite his reputation
as the remover of obstacles,
Ganesha clutches lotus flower,
tasty pastry and scepter,
chubby body trapped
within block of granite.

His eight arms are cramped
as he enfolds bare-breasted stone women.
It's all he can do to clutch staff and mace.
Phallic trunk curled, slit eyes stare
toward museum tourists, possibly heaven.

Gawky boys pass and point,
awkward in adolescence,
trapped between child and man,
betrayed by their own
grotesque bodies.

BLISS

Asian Art Museum, San Francisco, July 2015

Vishnu clasps a gold, multi-armed goddess
who straddles his lap in a lusty embrace.
Despite gilt garments,
they kiss, erotically entangle,
bound to the wheel of sensual bliss.

Voyeuristic visitors glance,
consult museum brochures, discreetly move on.
Inspired lovers look and learn,
seek a quiet corner,
feel themselves blaze.

Blood Moon Eclipse

Fog cloaks the dark deed,
permits meager pearl glow
to escape from consumed lunar face.

Earth's shadow advances,
tugs emotions off-kilter.
Planets realign; hidden faults shudder.

Celestial tsunami casts
impenetrable enigma over light,
Artemis assaulted, despoiled.

Estuary Etching

Sepia sunrise radiates over bronzed cove.
Park bench and feathery cypress
frame a daguerreotype scene.

An empty trail winds
from Lover's Point to Fisherman's Wharf,
ends at Del Monte Beach.

Morning scalds placid water.
On dry boulders, harbor seals doze.
Silver pelicans squabble.

Laconic surf sluices ashore,
deposits broken shells, uprooted seaweed,
tangled snarls of kelp.

I savor private epiphany—
biting breeze, skidding sailboats,
azure expanse of wave pleated bay.

Exorcism

Sunrise lacerates chill morning mist.
Anchored fishing boats veer with the tide,
inscribe ephemeral arcs upon silver bay.

Gossiping gulls dissect toppled trash,
flap in outrage at larcenous black birds
who pilfer French fries, cheeseburger wrappings.

A trail interrupted by puddles
circumscribes Monterey harbor.
Recent rains revive dormant sedge.
Lacy spiderwebs sparkle.

Showers restore faith, lift the heart,
resurrect mummified yarrow.

Rouge

"Red sky at night, sailors' delight...."

El Niño simmers offshore, tarts up rouged horizon.
Approaching storm front announces itself
with brutal tides, crumbling coastline.

Rain clouds churn aloft over turbulent ocean.
Gnawed beach is devoured.
Morning frost disappears, supplanted by drizzle.

Hands and hips ache,
foretell coming moisture.
Wind rises. Abused pine trees groan.

GLEANING

Leftover clusters of mummified grapes
dangle from denuded branches.
Sparse scalded leaves detach,
drift to earth, crumble to compost.

Autumn's lush harvest—zinfandel,
blushing grenache, chubby red globe—
have been gathered for jelly or wine crush.
Second-best leavings sustain blackbird beggars.

I glean metaphors from dying vines,
shriveled raisins and petrified tendrils,
scribble poetry of coming frost, blasted canes,
sweet fruit's dormant buds.

MORNING ON MOONSTONE BEACH

Pelicans scout collapsing spindrift.
Overhead, impending storm festers.

Beneath greasewood—squirrels,
sparrows, cautious cottontail bunnies.

High tide retreats, reveals broken shells,
uprooted seaweed, driftwood.

A lone surfer descends from ragged bluff,
flings board and himself into violent ocean.

White caps punctuate restless sea,
frame a fishing procession of giant blue herons.

About the Author

Jennifer Lagier has published ten books of poetry. Her poems have appeared in a variety of national and international literary magazines and anthologies. She taught with California Poets in the Schools and is now a retired college librarian/instructor. Jennifer is a member of the Italian American Writers Association and Rockford Writers Guild. She co-edits the *Homestead Review* and maintains websites for *Ping Pong: A Literary Journal of the Henry Miller Library*, *The Monterey Poetry Review*, and misfitmagazine.net. She also helps coordinate the Monterey Bay Poetry Consortium's Second Sunday Reading Series and designs the chapbook for the Blue Light Press Summer Writing Workshop. Visit her website at: www.jlagier.net.